T0103032

MAKING THE MOST OF EACH DAY IN LIFE

Beryl Maureen Hammond

Copyright © 2007 by Beryl Maureen Hammond.

Library of Congress Control Number: 2006910095

ISBN: Hardcover   978-1-4257-2352-1
               Softcover   978-1-4257-2351-4

All rights reserved. No part of this book may be reproduced or transmitted in any form or by any means, electronic or mechanical, including photocopying, recording, or by any information storage and retrieval system, without permission in writing from the copyright owner.

This book was printed in the United States of America.

To order additional copies of this book, contact:
Xlibris Corporation
1-888-795-4274
www.Xlibris.com
Orders@Xlibris.com
33714

CONTENTS

ACKNOWLEDGEMENTS

For A Short Book,
A Long List Of Credits

As I began to think of all the people to whom I would like to express my appreciation for their support and hard work in making this book possible, the list continued to grow.

I wish to thank the whole team at Xlibris Corporation. For a wonderful team at Xlibris, without them it would be impossible to do what I do. Thank you all for tying it all together.

To my Publishing Consultant, Jerry Valencia, thank you for pushing me forward and the phone calls you made. I know I am laid back, thanks for the push.

To Greg Haigh a Publishing Consultant at Xlibris Corporation. Thanks also to Kennedy Salvo, Submissions Representative.
To Lynnel Landerito, Submissions Representative.
To Sherwin Soy my Cover Design Specialist. Thanks, you did a great job.
To sweetie Guzman, my Marketing Services Representative.
To Stephanie Ong, Author Services Representative.
To Kathrina Garcia, Manuscript Service Specialist

Then, of course, there were the combined efforts of the outstanding editing by Ava Marie A. Villareal.

I wish to thank a mentor, Dr. Selete Avoke for overseeing the writing and giving me helpful pointers. You kept me laughing.

Thanks also to Augustine Baffo for all the errands and for always coming to my rescue, for his good nature and unflagging help throughout the process and for going the extra mile and always being there.

To Catherine Hermano and her family. Rudy, Julian and Claudia, whose home I started writing this book. Thank you for creating an environment where I could let the creative juices flow at any hour of the day or night and have my ideas received by sympathetic ears. Thank you Cathy for suggesting that I write this book and for believing in me.

To the teachers whose personalities, methods and friendships have affected me most—Professor Larry Kortering and Pat Braziel of Appalachian State University, Professor Augustine Esogbue of Georgia Technical Institute, Professor Asante-Poku University of Ghana Medical School. You can never be forgotten.

A great big hug of thanks to all of my wonderful and diversified contributors and friends Philip, Evelyn, David Aasan, Kay, Lenard, you are awesome, Emmanuel, Elizabeth, Ayisha, Demi, Naa, Jennifer, Charles, Jeffrey, Bantus, Joanna, Roberta, Robert, Kodwo, K.S, Paul, Max Vardon, Emelia, Valerie, Naomi, Selasi, Edem and Benedicta.

Above all to my Father and Mother.

INTRODUCTION

This book is designed for you to take information, decide what you think is useful, and apply it accurately to your life and throw away what you find doesn't work. However, try the principles before you judge them. I have offered some quotes, so you can derive whatever value may be found. As with all human uttering, some conclusions may be debatable and some sources dubious. Nevertheless, I believe truth is truth, however questionable the voice which utters them; thus, I will not debate on them; instead, I invite you to enjoy and learn whatever you can from these.

When you are born, you are given life to live and accept wholeheartedly whatever life offers. *Death and life are in the power of the tongue: and they that love it shall eat the fruit there of. Proverbs 18:21* In life, there are so many choices you have to make. Some of these choices can determine your future or where you will get to or how far you will go in life. Life is not easy and fair, but if you make the right choice, it will be good to you. It's important to focus on the choice you make. In focusing on your choice, you have to belief and have faith in the choice you make. In doing that, you have to put your ideas into action. Only action supported by life will be sustained long enough to produce results. Life is moving; you need to steer yourself in a direction you have predetermined. With faith, strategy, passion, persistence, perseverance, belief, commitment, and energy, you will come out with successful results in life. With your passion and the pragmatic determination, success is on the horizon. Commitment is very important because it is the quality of commitment that separates good from great, and there is no abiding success without commitment. Then you get the power to change your life, to shape your perceptions, to make things work for you and not against you.

If you accept my words and store up my commands within you, turning your ear to wisdom and apply your heart to understanding, and if you call out for insight and cry aloud for understanding, and if you look for it as for silver and search for it as for hidden treasure, then you will understand the fear of the LORD and find the knowledge of God. For the LORD gives wisdom, and from his mouth come knowledge and understanding. Proverbs 2:1-6

SECTION I

The Greatest Power We Have Within

LIFE AND CHOICES

I have known her all my life. She lived under the shadow of her wealthy father for twenty-four years. After college, she decided to move away from her father. She left for another continent with nothing. At first, it seemed to her like an adventure, to leave all the mansion, money, wealth, and happiness for another continent more than ten hours away by air.

It all seemed so incredible, and yet the thing that amazed me most was that I realized that she is me! "Her" story is my own. It was a choice I made. We all have the freedom to choose; we just need the courage to follow our own path. The power to transform our lives into our greatest dreams lies waiting within us all. It's time to unleash it! In this present age, many people are able to achieve wondrous things almost overnight.

What makes the difference in the life we lead? They are our actions and choices we take. Two people could go through the same or similar experiences in life, but they will both act or react in different ways. That is what makes the difference. If a couple had developed a successful marriage where for thirty years they still felt deeply in love with each other, I could find out what actions they had taken and the beliefs they had that created that result; and I could adopt them and produce the same or similar results.

Chart a course for your future and how you want to lead your life. Think of life as a road map—first, choose your destination, and then think about the best possible route of how to arrive at your chosen destination. Trust your gut instincts, but don't forget to put your analytical skills to work, too. Take responsibility for choices you make. You have to live with the path you choose. Whatever it is that you decide to do, make sure it works. It will involve a lot of sacrifice. Make it look like your whole life depends on it. Make choices that make sense for your unique and individual needs. It's best to see situations from all sides. Meditate on important goals in life. Write out your goals and keep it somewhere where you will see it all the time to serve as a constant reminder. It could be hung on the wall in your bedroom or at the bedside or boldly written on a wall. For a goal, which is not written, is only a wish, and as we know, not all wishes come to pass.

The future is a complete unknown. As much as you prepare for what you think might or should happen, you can never really predict the course of events. Even the wisest do not even know the end. The unexpected may pop up; always be conscious and know how to handle it.

Start now to spend some time thinking through your likes and dislikes so that when you begin to make important life decisions, you know what you want. For example, know what type of environment you want to work or live, things *that make you happy or sad, whether you want to be a chief executive officer of a small business or a receptionist in a prestigious enterprise, the qualities you admire in other people,* subjects you enjoy studying. Does it matter that you study subjects you enjoy and eventually work in a career area that you like? Or study subjects that you think will enable you to earn more income but then you have no interest in? When I was a little girl, my passion was to draw and paint. Before six years, I could draw and paint everybody in the family. Everyone was so proud of me except my dad. I would sit down and draw for hours without food or drink. My dad stopped me from painting and drawing, and I became so unhappy. He always wanted me to study medicine, and he was disappointed when I studied business in college. In high school,

I discovered I had the passion for writing. My favorite books were M&B and romance novels, and I would write stories of how I wanted my life to be.

Life is God's gift to you. What you do with your life is your gift to God. Live your life with a purpose, for nothing that has already taken place can be changed. The best you can do is to learn from your experience and other people's experience and use that knowledge to make improvements and better choices in situations you encounter. You don't have to be in Rome to know what happens in Rome; take time to read broadly and gather experience.

Anything that you are addicted to doing and on a regular basis constitutes a habit. Your habit might be eating junk food, watching soap operas instead of studying, leaving your room tidy, etc. Your habits reveal a lot about you, and they can prevent you from reaching your goal. For example, if your goal is to pass all your exams, and you have a habit of gossiping or staying out late to watch movies, your goal of studying to pass your exams will not come to pass.

Watch your thoughts, for *they become your words. Choose your words, for they become actions. Understand your actions, for they become habits. Study your habits, for they will become your character. Develop your character, for it becomes your destiny. In the same way our thoughts affect our decisions, our decisions affect our actions; our actions affect our habits; our habits affect our character, and our character affects our destiny. Our thoughts shape our decisions; our decisions shape our actions; our action shapes our habits; our habit shapes our character, and our character shapes our destiny.*

When you sow a thought, you reap a deed, sow a deed and reap a habit, sow a habit and reap a character, sow a character and reap a destiny. Your destiny starts in your thought of life. To reap good things, sow good things. If you want God to solve your problems, go out there and solve other people's problems. When you meet other people's need, God will meet yours. When you make other people happy, you will be happy.

Be not deceived, God is not mocked; for whatever a man sowed, that shall he also reap. Galatians 6:7

Each man is responsible for his own character. If character did determine a man's destiny then every man created his own heaven or hell. We are each the authors of our own lives; we live in what we have created.

Life is all about choices. Every situation is a choice; you can choose how you will react to situations and people. To be happy or to be unhappy is your choice. Learn how to act and react appropriately and spontaneously in every situation. Do not overact or overreact; do not attack or contend, and you will be protected. You will receive from each situation what is yours, not more or less. Every situation in life is an opportunity to use this great power of mental rehearsal.

Everyone on earth is free to use their great powers of creation in whatever way they want. Everyone is creating their own circumstances in life whether they know it or not. Everyone is a creator of his/her own destiny. It is up to us as individuals to be the master of our own mind, to accumulate great wealth and create the manner of living that we dream of, and making our dreams into goals. In order to create great wealth, we must become aligned with positive energy.

Life is a journey, and we need to sow a seed in life today and reap tomorrow. As a Christian, I know a seed is something that blesses somebody, like love, peace, forgiveness, responsibility, goodwill, patience, and giving. Giving certainly does not have to cost anything at all. Oftentimes we get so caught up in the commercialism *of giving that we soon find ourselves stressing out our spending. Yet if we take a deep breath and reflect on giving, we find that we can give in nonmaterial ways . . . a hug and a heartfelt letter of appreciation and even a homemade gift of cookies.* There is an example in Ruth 13:7-8. Naomi was all alone because her husband and two sons had died. She wanted each of her daughters-in-law to find a new husband. But Ruth loved her mother-in-law so much that she chose to stay with Naomi. Ruth showed her love by being loyal to Naomi. I hope these little suggestions help you as much as it does me!

BEING HAPPY WHERE YOU ARE IN LIFE

As I was going through this phase, I just remembered that when it's all done and when it will matter most, God will not compromise quality. His tea will be of the brand name "BERYL." A potential winner "they say" is like a tea bag. It is not worth much until it has been through some hot water.

In everyone's life, there comes a time of ultimate challenge—a time when every resource we have is tested. A time when our faith, our belief, our values, our patience are all pushed to our limits. Some people see such test as opportunities and *preparation for greatness, and they use that to become better people—others allow these experiences of life to destroy them.*

We all go through problems and challenges in life, whether you are rich, poor, wealthy, beautiful, colored, powerful, or great. The difference is how we respond to life's challenges. There are so many people in this world who live such joyous lives in spite of almost every adversity, while others who would seem to have it all live lives of despair, depression, and anger. Be happy where you are in life, in whatever situation you find yourself.

As you continue to change and grow throughout your life, your desires change as well. Lead a lifestyle that will make you happy. Your ideal lifestyle is whatever would make you the happiest, not what fits the norm or what would make other people happy. Try and figure out what satisfies you, challenges you, and spurs your creativity.

Apart from sleep, what we do more in our lives is working. We spend approximately forty-five years working, five days a week, eight hours a day. When you don't like your work, you will not like your life either, because you spend most of your time working.

Look to this day! For it is life, the very life of life. In it's brief course lie all the verities and realities of your existence; the bliss of growth, the glory of action, the splendor of beauty, for yesterday is but a dream and tomorrow is only a vision but today well-lived makes every yesterday a dream of happiness, and every tomorrow a vision of hope. Look well therefore to this day!

—From the Sanskrit

It is commonly believed that anyone who possesses lots of wealth and money is happy. Because of this, many people are struggling so hard to acquire wealth and find happiness. Jesus however said that a man's life does not consist of the abundance of things he possess (Luke 12:15). John the Baptist possessed neither earthly wealth nor goods and yet Jesus described him as the greatest man of his day (Matt 11:11).

Jesus spoke a parable unto his disciples saying the ground of a certain rich man brought forth plentifully. And he thought within himself, saying, What shall I do, because I have no room where to bestow my fruits? And he said, this will I do: I will pull down my barns, and build greater: and there will I bestow all my fruits and my goods. And I will say to my soul, soul, thou hast much, much goods laid up for many years. Take thine easy eat, drink and be merry. But God said unto him, thou fool, this night thy soul shall be required of thee: then whose shall things be, which thou hast provided? (Luke12: 16-20)

Life is a journey, and you need to enjoy life where you are. We take for granted what we have. One funny thing about life is the most you get is what you ask for. When you are selling your house for $10,000, no one will offer $20,000 because that is not what you asked for.

Be yourself; be what God wants you to be and what you want to be. Trying to be like other people steals your joy and peace. Let us pray to God to get that junk out of our lives. Do not try to be what you are not; do not try to be what your family, friends, and society want you to be. Be willing to take advice, but you have to be free to be you. You will be cheating yourself if you try to please people. You cannot satisfy everybody in this world, and not everybody can appreciate what you do. For if you think you can satisfy everybody, you will end up satisfying no one. Do things on your own without worrying about what others expect from you. Your physical energy could be riding high; it is time to tackle overdue projects.

Be careful who you allow to influence you. Most of the decisions you make, do not listen to people; they will want you to do things their way, in a manner that will benefit them. Do what you feel good about. Do not do what people are doing. You have to be original. People will let you do things their way, but you have to do it your way. You have to walk in your own anointing; it's not important what you have, but whether it has God's anointing. Do not copy anybody just to be you. Be what God made you to be. Do not try to be something that you are not; enjoy how you are and what God made you to be, and be the best you can. Find peace, joy, and happiness from within.

God parted the water of the Red Sea so that Moses and the Israelite slaves could escape from Egypt. Once they had safely crossed to the other side of the sea, the Israelites realized that they were free at last! Miriam was so full of joy that she started to dance and sing (Exodus 15:20).

Enjoy the people in your life; enjoy your work, life, family, and everything around you. Become interested in your environment and general surroundings, taking pride in their appearances and *neatness. People are stressed out, both at home and on the job. In these times, you need to be more sociable and mingle.*

You may need to get plenty of fresh air as a rule, and especially if you are in an environment that is stuffy; try to" unstuffy" it!

There was a time that I was teaching kids at Sunday school, and the topic was "stresses." I then asked each of them to tell me some of the stressful situations they go through. One said, "Am stressed when I have to do my homework." Another said, "Am stressed when I have to take my bath in the morning." Will you call the Lord in the days when you are stressed? "I called upon the Lord in distress; the Lord answered me, and set me in a large place" (Psalm 118:5). *We often try to ignore our pains by drinking alcohol, having sex outside of marriage, buying nice things for ourselves, trying to make ourselves happy, attending services, etc. All of these cannot drown our pains. We can only receive the miraculous power of God only if we believe in his son Jesus Christ. Not by reading the Bible enough, going to church enough, or being good enough.*

Do not seek to recall yesterday that is past, nor repine for tomorrow, which has not yet come; do not build your hopes on the past or the future. Be happy now and do not live on wind.—Omar Khayyám

All emotions are natural and have their purpose, even the ones that we may not feel proud of. I understand how it can be, but it is a fact. Sometimes being alone can be very renewing. This is a time for decision. Your intellect and personal instincts will serve you well. In relationships of all kinds, you make your needs and positions clearly understood. Whatever mood you are in will be uniquely your own, as everything you do is unique. Your personal freedom includes being able to change your mood as you wish.

A pastor disliked his wife that he wanted her dead. Since God is against divorce, all he could wish for was for his wife to die. On Sundays, while preaching, his wife would be selling merchandise on the church premises, and he felt so embarrassed. This pastor is a man of God. I am not judging him, but I think that despite his wife's behavior, he was supposed to show love to his wife, to love her sacrificially, purposefully, unconditionally as he loves his own body. A wife is a gift from God, and you are to spend the rest of your life with her and grow old together. The meaning of love in marriage means

Listen to your wife, look at her in the eye, and let her express how she feels about a situation.

Open up, speak up, and let her know what is happening in your life.

Visualize by putting yourself in her shoes, and knowing what she goes through.

Encourage her. Tell her how special she is; tell her genuinely; she may know it but tell her.

Think much about the love of Christ. What compels and constrains your life? What is it that motivates your life? Is it the love of Christ?

You could lose your job; though it seems bad, it forces you to dig deeper into yourself for courage and resourcefulness. When your marriage or relationship breaks up, it makes you face being alone, and it leads to more independence and prepares you for a better relationship in the future.

I lost somebody that I loved so dearly at a time that I was preparing for my GMAT exams. I thought all my dreams had been shattered. I felt that I had lost everything that was so dear to me. All along, I thought love alone was enough in a relationship. I thought that was the end of my world. I then took this giant image of "this is the end of me" that I had created in my mind and literally shrank it down to size, and then I began to set up a new set of representations about what I could do. I changed my belief systems. That night when I was going to bed, I asked God to take the hurt and bitterness from me and replace it with joy, peace, and happiness. It worked like magic. What did I do from there? I started looking at the positive side of it all. I dug deeper into myself for courage and resourcefulness. It made me face being alone, led me to be more independent, and I asked God to prepare me for a better relationship in the future. It was when the relationship ended that I got to know so many negative things about him. I look back today and realize that ending the relationship did me so much good.

Before you fall in love, ask yourself whether this person will handicap you emotionally or spiritually. Let's look at love. From a modeling point of view, love is a state, and like all states, all results, it is produced by specific sets of actions or stimuli when they are perceived or represented in certain ways. One of the most important perceptual ingredients of falling in love is associating with all the things you like or don't like about the person. Falling in love can be such a heady, disorienting feeling because it's not a balanced one. You are not making a balanced sheet of a person's good and bad qualities. You're totally associated with a few elements of another person you find intoxicating.

Love is caring so much for other people that it shows in the way you treat them. Love is more that a warm feeling; it is acting unselfishly for another's good. When you are full of love, you choose to act with kindness, patience, and forgiveness. You show your love by the things that you do or say. It's easy to love other people when they are kind and friendly. It's much harder when they are rude or selfish. But no matter how they act, you show your love for them by treating them kindly, fairly, and with understanding.

Relationship requires investment of time and physical and psychological, emotional energy. Some require more energy. Before you enter a relationship, understand the person. Understand the person's history. Know what she went through during childhood, both good and bad times. Understand and know the person well. Know his or her history before dealing with him or her. When dealing with someone, know the person's objective and yours as well.

Everybody that treats you nicely does not necessarily want a relationship with you. And the fact that somebody is rude and harsh does not mean that person does not want a relationship. He may be having a hard time trying to settle bills. Unless you are special, most people don't want to deal with you. Some people may want to deal with you because they want a favor. There is a bit of confusion in the world because people may want a relationship but then are dealing with people who are looking for relations, to use you, get what they want, and get rid of you. You may want a relationship and end up with a person who only wants a relation.

It will cost us everything to be in a relationship. It will cost us time; we will have to sacrifice our personal interest. We may have to spend our money on others. When money and wealth and material things are gone, what will not go is relationship with friends and others. Let us be careful so we don't lose all our relationships because of money. Let us aim at having the kind of relationship David had with Jonathan. In your time of abundance, share with your friends and invest in them.

Before you start a relationship with someone, know the person's goal, objectives, and ascertain his or her expectation; ask yourself what you require and expect. You need to be motivated to establish a relationship with someone. It is very tough to be with a person who does not treat you right. You could be in a relationship with someone and the person will be pretending. I don't need any drama, I've had enough already; I don't know about you. For some people, you see it right away that it is all drama.

Before starting a relationship, it's necessary to know yourself, be aware of your preferences, and have some standards. Reveal and articulate who you like and what you like. Be honest, truthful, and tell it like it is. People need to have their eyes wide open before entering a relation. Don't trick your partner, and don't act like you're straight when you're not. Let the person know who you really are and accept you for who you are in a relationship; there must be mutual admiration with respect.

We all have a supreme value, the one thing we most desire from any situation, whether it's a relationship or a job. It may be freedom; it may be love; it may be excitement, or it may be security. You probably read the list and said to yourself, "I want all those things." Most of us do. But we put a relative value on them all. What one person wants from a friendship is ecstasy; another, love; a third, honest communication; a fourth, a sense of security. Most people are totally unaware of their hierarchies, of those of their loved ones. They have a vague sense of wanting love, or challenge or ecstasy, but they don't have a sense of how these pieces fit together. These distinctions are absolutely critical. They determine whether or not a person's ultimate needs will be met. You can't fill someone else's needs if you don't know what they are. You can't help someone do the same for you, and you can't deal with your own conflicting values, until you understand the hierarchies in which they are interacting.

Friendship is built on similarities, and you can't call anyone a best friend unless he or she calls you his or her best friend too. It's a sad but natural process: when one's friend's life situation changes, so does the friendship. Change is progress, not betrayal.

What ruins a relationship? Many factors, one may be that you no longer associate with the things that attracted you to that person in the first place. Sometimes, the other party is no longer consistently applying a specific thing that triggers that feeling.

People have certain value that when violated causes them to leave a relationship. For example, if support is number 1 on a person's value list, but he doesn't feel supported, he may end the relationship. Someone else who ranks support as third or fourth or fifth, and love as first, won't leave the relationship no matter what happens—as long as he feels loved.

If you place a value on romance, you might say your evidence procedure is to have a good relationship with an attractive and loving woman. That's a reasonable outcome worth pursuing. You may even have a clear picture of the looks and personality traits you most want. That's fine, too. Another may have a tempestuous romance with a blond blue-eyed with a forty-two-inch bust, who lives in Fifth Avenue condo in Manhattan, and a six-figure income. There is nothing wrong with having a target, but there is great deal of frustration if you link your values to a picture that's too specific.

You're ruling out 99 percent of the people or experiences that could satisfy you. That doesn't mean you can't create. What matters most to you in an intimate relationship? I've listed an example below.

Love
Mutual communication
Respect
Ecstasy
Growth
Support
Spiritual unity
Fun
Challenge
Creativity
Honesty
Attraction
Beauty
Freedom

These are not all the important values. You may find some values more important than the ones listed here.

In any relationship, whether it's as intense as it is between a father and son or as casual as it is between two salespeople sharing the same phone, you have a contract, whether you verbalize it or not. You both expect certain things from each other. You both judge each other's actions and words, at least unconsciously, by your values. You might as well get clear on what those values are and create agreements so that you know in advance how your behaviors will affect you both and what your true needs are.

Jesus was having dinner one evening when "tax collectors and sinners came and sat down with Him" (Matthew 9:10). The religious leaders of that day were outraged by his behavior. Their conclusion was that Jesus was a friend of sinners, and as it turns out, he was. "The son of man has come to seek and to save that which was lost" (Luke 19:10).

Jesus was morally separated from sinners and never took part in their lifestyle. Yet he did not separate himself physically from sinful people. He spent time with them and became their friend.

Just like Jesus, you and I can't help but rub shoulders with all kinds of people in our daily activities, not with the intension of taking part in their lifestyle, but helping them and being there for them. Contrast that self-serving attitude with the genuine friendship Jesus showed us. He said, "Greater love has no one than this, than to lay down ones life for his friends" (John 15:13). Then he demonstrated self-sacrificing love for us by dying on the cross to forgive our sins.

Tertullian, an early Roman writer, described the relationships between the Christians and non-Christians of his day this way: "We live among you, eat the same food, and wear the same clothes . . . We sojourn with you in the world, renouncing neither forum, nor market, nor bath, nor booth, nor workshop, nor inn . . . We till the ground with you, we join with you in business ventures."

We too must seek the lost, as Jesus did—and it doesn't take much effort. It's good to ask ourselves from time to time, "How many friends do I have who are lost?"

Lead me to some soul today, o teach me, Lord, just what to say; friends of mine are lost in sin and cannot find their way.—Houghton

When we trust Jesus as our savior and learn to obey him, we experience a deep friendship that gives reality and sincerity to the friendliness we show to others.

Lord, help us to avoid the shallow friendliness that uses others to get what we want. Teach us instead to radiate the warmth of genuine Christ like friendliness to everyone we meet.—Dave Egner

If friendship is genuine, it surely will convey a warm and caring attitude in all we do and say.—D. De Haan

Our world has so many people who need just one act of love to change their lives. These people may not think they fit in, or they may be facing turmoil that makes them feel all alone. Sometimes all we need to do is extend a hand, offer a smile, or speak a word of encouragement. As believers, we know and experience the love of God (John 3:16), so we are especially able to reach out to people and share that love.

There are enough people to go around so that everyone can have friends. Let's take the initiative to make sure no one is left out.—Dave Branon

I went outside to find a friend but could not find one there; I went outside to be a friend, and friends were everywhere!—Payne

A bad time brings good people around. Most times when you are going through bad times, friends can come in all shapes and sizes, even friendly faces in the animal world. Being part of a group can bring new meaning to everyday activities—have fun, my dear. Friends will urge that you break from routine and play. Make sure a few hours of fun will not spoil weeks of work on an important project. If you are in the mood to sit back and do nothing, I say, "Why not!" Appearances can mislead—even if you do not look busy on the outside, you may be processing a lot inside. Enthusiasm is apt to spread, so start the ball rolling.

The point am trying to make is that no matter what you are going through, turn it around. It could be negative but look at the positive side of it and be happy. When climbing a mountain, sometimes you have to go back a step in order to climb higher. No matter the situation you are in, you have to be happy right where you are. Develop great freedom of action that will encourage you to be happy in any situation.

Do what makes you truly happy. There is radiance in the face of a woman who takes joy in her life.—Sylvie Chantecaille

Get ready to bring stability back into your life. This influence will get your head out of the clouds and plant your feet on solid ground. Confidence can be your motto, as you feel you can handle anything. There will probably be very little you cannot accomplish once you set your mind on it.

Create your own happiness. If no one can make you happy, make yourself happy. Know where your interest is and create happiness for yourself. You could stumble on a delightful garden or park while you are out for a walk. Stay there for a while and enjoy the quiet and beauty of the place. Breathe in the air and find a bit of happiness. If the walls are pushing in on you, just call upon the Lord, and he will push away the walls. We need to leave situations like this for God to take care of. How you feel is not the result of what is happening in your life, it is your interpretation of what is happening.

Sometimes we ask God why he did not answer a prayer. We need to trust God in all situations. Sometimes we ask God for something, and he gives something else, which might not be what you expect. Whatever it is, just accept it because God knows best. Sometimes we trust God because we want him to do it our way. We need to trust God even if the answer is not what we are looking for. The true test of our faith comes when we get what we are not looking for. His ways are better and higher than ours are. The whys of life will not lead you to victory. God closes the wrong doors, and he has got you in the palm of his hands; let God do it his way. He knows what the best is for us. We need to trust him. All things work for good for those that love the Lord.

All things work for good for those who love God and are called according to His purpose (Romans 8:28).

We all go through things that are not fair, and sometimes we keep asking ourselves questions. We do not have all the answers.

The truth is there are some things we cannot fix. If you are going to trust God, you must understand God is a God of justice. Your situation may not be fair, but God is fair. Do not allow things to drag you down and steal your destiny. God will pay back the people who hurt you; just keep your heart pure.

Vengeance is mine; I will repay, saith the Lord.—Romans 12:19b

God is at work in your life whether you see it or not. Your situation may be the same, but God is at work. Even though we see nothing happening, God is working behind the scene. There is an appointed time, meaning there is a right time. God can see the big picture. There is no such thing as a coincidence with the work of our God. In a split second of time, God can bring everything to pass, and suddenly things will begin to change. Keep doing your best. God is making things happen even if you do not realize it. Do your best to stay in the rest of God. The point am making is that God is in control; he knows from the beginning to the end. If it's God's time, it does not matter what is happening in the natural. Human nature is to have everything right now. God has an appointed time to bring our dreams into being.

To everything there is a season, and a time to every purpose under the heaven.—Ecclesiastes 3:1

I will instruct you and teach you in the way you should go; I will counsel you and watch over you.—Psalm 32:8

Life is a very short trip. While alive, live.—Malcolm Forbes

You have to enjoy every stage of your life no matter the situation; we need to let God solve our problems.

Sometimes we think life is short; the problem is not life being short, but we wait too long. We wait too long to put ideas into action. You need to set goals and reach them one after the other. Make the most of each day. There is no end to what you can do. There is nothing you can do about yesterday. Learn from yesterday, live for today, and hope for tomorrow. You need to be enthusiastic with all that you do. Live each day to the fullest. Get the most you can get before the day ends.

Leave nothing for tomorrow, which can be done today.—Abraham Lincoln

Yet a little sleep, a little slumber, a little folding of the heads to sleep; so shall thy poverty come as one that traveled and thy want as an armed man.—Proverbs 6:10-11

If you were sick for long and got well, or recovered from the illness, you will be the happiest being existing. Sometimes we ask ourselves questions like "what shall I wear today?" "what shall I fix for dinner?" but you know what? Ethiopians do not have to worry about what to fix for dinner because all they have is bean and filthy water in the morning and night. No problem with what to wear, only a filthy dress to wear for a day, month, or perhaps for the whole year. Nevertheless, Ethiopians are exceedingly thankful to God. Some of us do not thank God because of the vast extensiveness of his bounty. If you are thankful to God for your wife, you will not commit adultery; if you appreciate what you have, you will not steal. God's delays for our request are not denials. We wake up and begin our daily chores without kneeling to pray. As a matter of fact, we do not even bless our meals or pray before going to bed. We are so unthankful, and that is what the devil likes about us. In all things, give thanks to God.

Look at the birds of the air, they do not sow or reap or store away barns, and yet your heavenly father feeds them. Are you not much more valuable than they? Who by worrying can add a single hour to his life? And why do you worry about clothes? See how the lilies of the fields grow. They do not labor or spin. Yet I tell you that

not even Solomon in all his splendor was dressed like one of these.
If that is how God clothes the grass of the field, which is here today
and tomorrow is thrown into the fire, will he not much more clothe
you, o you of little faith? (Matthew 6:26-30).

Problems tend to resolve themselves when they are not met
with aggression or impulsive action but are instead met head-on
and are solved in a respectful, harmonious way.

Whenever I start something new, I like to remind myself to let
go of the things I can't control, which turns out to be everything
that is outside myself! When I try to control what other people
think or do, or the circumstances that are going on around me, I
find the only thing that happens is that I waste a lot of my energy
that could be put to better use. So instead of driving yourself nuts
by trying to be in control of the world—concentrate on what is in
your control, like your desires, your opinions, and your emotions.
The rest will take care of itself.

Jesus said, "I tell you, do not worry about your life, what you
will eat; or about your body, what you will wear. Life is more than
food, and the body more than clothes."—Luke 12:22-23

We all have a reason to be happy. When did you last thank
God for the ability to see and the ability to hear? You have to
learn to be happy right where you are. Life may not be what you
expect, but you need to make the most of it. Sometimes I say to
myself that if I could sing, then my life will be much better. I
like singing, but then I do not sing because I know the lyrics of
the song, but because the song has extended to my heart.

The only way you can accomplish that is by blooming
wherever you are. Your environment should not keep you from
being happy. You need to quit trying to change things you cannot
change, like being in traffic or changing the behavior of another
person. Be happy where you are and keep a good attitude; be

faithful and content. If you do not bloom now, you will be complaining, and situations will not get better.

It is not important where you are but where you are going and whether you are performing and bearing fruits. People may think that you have to be in America to make it in life, but they have the wrong perception of America. If you are not happy where you are, you will never get to where you want to be in life. You have to be content; being content means being happy where you are and being grateful for what God has done. If thankful, your life will be better. We need to be grateful even in the imperfect world. The Bible condemns ungratefulness as a seminal sin. Nothing is going to be perfect in this world because we live in a cursed world of sin. Sometimes one might think that he does not have to thank God because he worked hard to buy the bread. But that is wrong, because behind the bread is the baker; behind the baker is the miller; behind the miller is the farmer; behind the farmer is sunshine and rainfall; behind sunshine and rainfall is "God."

We all go through things that are not fair. Why did my love go down? Why did I fail? We do not have all the answers. The truth is there are certain things we cannot fix. You might not have control over the storm, but you have control over the boat. If you are going to trust God, you are going to understand God that he is a God of justice. Your situation may not be fair, but God is fair. The whys of life open the door of anger and bitterness. Do not allow things to drag you down and steal your destiny. Remember that everything needs your permission to make you angry. God will pay back the people who hurt you, but keep your heart pure. Our attitude should be, God I will serve you whether I understand a situation or not, whether my prayers are answered or not. I am going to serve you whether everything is perfect or not. I will trust you; even when I do not understand, that still will not change my faith. God's ways are not our ways. We all face things that do not make sense. Do not lean on your own understanding, but in all your ways, acknowledge the Lord, and he will direct your pathways.

WHAT IF . . . ?

- What if God couldn't take the time to bless us today because we could not take time to thank him yesterday?
- What if God decided not to lead us tomorrow because we did not follow him today?
- What if we never saw flower bloom because we grumbled when God sent the rain?
- What if God didn't walk with us today because we failed to recognize it as his day?
- What if God took away the Bible tomorrow because we would not read it today?
- What if God took away his message because we failed to listen to the messenger?
- What if God did not send his only begotten son because he wanted us to prepare to pay the price of sin?
- What if the door of the church was closed because we did not open the door of our hearts?
- What if God stopped loving and caring for us because we failed to love and care for others?
- What if God would not hear us today because we would not listen to him?
- What if God answered our prayers the way we answer his call to service?
- What if God met our needs the way we give him our lives?

IT TAKES ATTITUDE, NOT MONEY TO ENJOY LIFE

Attitude is your manner of acting, and it betrays your thinking and feeling. It affects everything you do and affects how you see yourself and your world. Attitude comes from the exposure of family, school, friends, and even the community. Despite that, you have the power to change your attitude through your life experiences. When I was growing up, I was so reserved and could not accept working with different kinds of people. Attending boarding school changed everything since we had to do things together and in groups. With time, I had no trouble surviving in an environment that promotes diversity.

Attitude will make or break a company, a church, a home, or a relationship. We have a choice daily regarding the attitude we embrace for the day. We cannot change our past. We cannot change the inevitable. The only thing we can do is play on the one string we have, and that is our attitude. We are in charge of our attitude.

It's a psychological fact that one's development means change in the person's self-concept. Each individual, whether we realize it or not, has a self-image. We see ourselves in some way—smart, intelligent, kindly, slow, well intentioned, lazy, misunderstood, meticulous, or shrewd; we all can pick adjectives that describe ourselves. This is the *I* behind the face of the mirror. The *I* that thinks, dreams, talks, feels, and believes, the *I* that no one knows fully. Everything we do or say, everything we hear, feel, or otherwise perceive, is influenced by how we see ourselves. How we see ourselves determines generally what we react to, what we perceive, and in broad terms, how we behave in general.

Each human being is several selves. A woman could be a mother, a wife, and a managing director of a firm. If there are conflicts among any of these roles, then discomfort arises. And such conflict brings with it such dynamics as tension and guilt. An example is when a woman is considered a good wife and a mother and a good business executive. She spends lots of time with her family, and suddenly, she finds the demands on her time overwhelming. Now what does she do? She can no longer be home to fix dinner for the family. She gets home from work very late, and the kids and her husband are already asleep. She leaves for the office early morning before the kids wake up. So what happens? She may feel deeply dissatisfied with such a necessity, and it may show in her behavior and attitude toward the people she deals with. Conflict between self-concept is a cause of ineffective behavior. By definition, the self-concept is an organization or patterning of attitudes, habits, knowledge, drives, and the like.

Our lives are not determined by what happens to us, but by how we react to what happens: not by what life brings to us, but by the attitude we bring to life. A positive attitude causes a chain reaction of positive thoughts, events, and outcomes. It is a catalyst . . . a spark that creates extraordinary results.

The Bible says, "Seek God alone in his righteousness and all things will be added unto you." These wise words make it very clear just how you should order your priorities in life. "A man's life consisted not in the abundance of the things that he possesses," (Luke 12:15). Do not be frustrated for what you have not achieved; make a decision to be happy where you are right now.

Keep your lives free from the love of money and be content with what you have, because God has said, "never will I leave you; never will I forsake you."—Hebrew 13:5

A believer is content with what he has in every stage of life, good or bad. Enjoy life in spite of circumstances. "Every house is built by some man; but he that built all things is God" (Hebrew 3:4). "Except the Lord build the house, they labor in vain that build it; except the Lord keep the city, the guard waketh but in vain" (Psalm 127:1). Money will not bring happiness. It makes you feel good. It may make life easy, but it will not bring happiness. It does not take money to enjoy life; it takes attitude. "For what shall it profit a man, if he shall gain the whole world, and lose his own soul?" (Mark 8:36)

Godliness with content is great gain. For we brought nothing into the world, and we can take nothing out of it. But if we have food and clothing, we will be content with that. People who want to get rich fall into temptation and a trap and into many foolish and harmful desires that plunge men into ruin and destruction. For the love of money is a root of all kinds of evil, some people eager for money, have wandered from the faith and pierced themselves with many grieves (1 Timothy 6:6-10).

Make the most of what you have and what God has given you. You have to learn to enjoy the simple things. Slow down and enjoy the simple things in life. Learn to have a good time; enjoy nature—the sea, rivers, trees, plants, etc.

Here's a secret that I find brings me a bit of happiness no matter what else may happen during my day. I make my bed every morning! I learned this in Achimota School. I have such a huge sense of accomplishment over this small act that I couldn't help but think, Hey, maybe there might be something to this. After doing this for sometime, I personally felt more organized and uplifted in the morning, and I liked coming home at the end of the day to a bed that looked inviting and cozy. And even if nothing else seemed to go right during the day, at least I had one accomplishment that made me feel good!

Most people live all stressed out. We should learn to have fun. You have to learn to slow down and enjoy life's journey. If you want to enjoy life, you have to live in the present, live one day at a time. God gives us what we need one day at a time. Enjoy every stage of your life.

Take part in-group activity; get together with friends, and do something special. Think about starting a walking club or joining a book lovers' circle, and depression will be managed.

There was a day when the prophet Elijah felt hopeless and wanted to die. He had just experienced a great victory over the prophets of Baal, but now the king's wife Jazebel was threatening his life. In fear, he ran into the wilderness (1 Kings 19:4). There he "prayed that he might die, and said, 'It's enough! Now, Lord, take my life!'"

We may think that Elijah was overreacting, but hopeless feelings are real. He wisely went to the right source for help—he cried out to God. The Lord knew Elijah needed restoration, so He provided for his needs (vv.15-17). God brought him hope by reminding him that he was not alone (v.18).

Look to God. He is your source of hope.—Anne Cetas

Lord, give us grace to trust You when life's burdens seem too much to bear; dispel the darkness with new hope and help us rise above despair.—Sper

BEING FOCUSED IN LIFE

One of the reasons men fail is broken focus. Focus on a dream that is within reach. It takes time for people to figure out their true purpose in life. You can dream of the rewards that go with hard work today, since you've given your all; now may be the time to kick back and take a holiday in which you treat yourself right and enjoy the finer things. Working on your own could give you a tremendous sense of satisfaction. Often when we really want something in our lives, we put all of our focus and energy toward trying to make it happen. But we may then find that no matter what we do, we get no closer to reaching it. These are the times when it feels like we are struggling against the universe. We have to let go and take a break.

When I realize that I am struggling against the universe, I take a deep breath and put my project aside. I do something nice for myself . . . I go for a walk, make a cup of tea, or get together with a friend. When I am ready to come back to my project, whether it's a few hours later or a few weeks later, I feel refreshed. I have a different perspective, and I've regained my enthusiasm; and magically my project moves forward with a sense of ease.

There are certain decisions that we make in life and regret, but then we have to know that there is no turning back. Everybody has made many mistakes in the past. Our greatest task will be to search the past to form the future, to begin an earnest search for a new and relevant set of values, and to learn to use the knowledge we have for the question that comes before us.

Whatever is behind us is done with and cannot be changed. Do not look behind; look ahead, and look in the future. Keep on climbing; keep on putting one foot before the other. There have been times in my life I picked up the treats of an old life; there are some pains that cannot be healed, so know that there is no turning back. Do not concentrate on how far the future is; just put one foot before the other. Do what you have to do in the present, and the future will take care of itself. God is the greatest planner; let us leave the future in his hands.

Life is not fair; we all do not have what we want to have. Make up your mind and go forward, and God will have a way of compensating you. If you do not spend the rest of your life with what you did not get, God will compensate you. God has something out there for you, and you have to know how to find it. Forget those things behind and reach for those ahead.

I know what I want, who I am, and would never ask for anything I could not give myself. I have a theory that the type of people you meet in your life serves as a compass for where you are headed in life. Example, if the people you are meeting have lives that are in terrible shape, then you are headed in the wrong direction. Nevertheless, on the same note, if the people you meet have lives that are turning in the right direction, and their future is brighter than their present, then you are surely on the right track. Therefore, with this in mind, you will meet the person you are truly meant to be with only when you have reached your peak. This is the same reason you seem to attract people whose lives are so similar to your own. If you feel good about who you are, and what you are in your life, there is no doubt you will attract positive people; but if you are unhappy and really down on yourself, you will attract those who are insecure and in need of reassurance.

If you associate yourself with people that are going places in life, then they are going to inspire you, and you are going to go further than you normally would have. Nevertheless, just the opposite is true; if you hang around lazy and undisciplined people, then before long, you are going to be lazy and undisciplined. If you are always around negative people, people that are constantly critical, people that are always finding faults, well, that is going to rub off on you; and you are going to be just like they are. If you hang around the barbershop long enough, you are going to get yourself a haircut.

The Bible says in Proverbs 13:20, when you walk with wise men, you will become wise, but a companion of fools will be destroyed. In other words, God is saying we are going to become exactly like the people that we are constantly around. I want to challenge you to examine your friendship, examine whom you are spending your time with. Ask yourself the question: do I want to be like this person? Do I like their quality? Do they inspire me to reach for new heights, or do they just drag me down, and get me all depressed? Do they have a vision for their life or just sitting back and settling for mediocrity?

You see too often that we do not really understand that the power of our friendship, the power of our association with others, could affect us. We think that we can be around whoever we want and not have it affect us but know that it is not true. It is affecting us, either good or bad. The Bible is very clear about whom we should not have close association with. It says do not have friendship with angry people, lazy people, people who talk too much, and people who are loose in morals. It is very critical whom we associate with. You may have a group of friends at work; you go to lunch with them every day, and they just sit around and gossip about everybody and everything. Talk about how bad the company is and talk about other people as well. Get away from those people and get out of that group. If you do not, it's going to get down into your spirit; and it will poison you. Find someone else to go out for lunch with. If you hang around them long enough, you are gong to become like a gossip just as they are. Do not sit there to allow it get into you.

If you have a hot-tempered friend who cannot control his anger, and you've tried several times trying to help him out and yet is not getting better, get away from him. Hot-tempered people are always getting into trouble; if you hang around them, it is going to come over you; before long, you are going to become hot tempered and going to get problems. Do not spend your time with people with bad attitude and always in trouble; do not let the devil deceive you into the wrong company that will steal your destiny. Do not worry about having most friends; the quantity of friends is not important but the quality. I would rather have one good friend that has his head on straight and going somewhere than I will have twenty-five friends doing what everyone else is doing.

A friend is a present you give yourself, and since you have the power to choose your friends, why don't you get yourself a big present? Why don't you choose a friend who will influence you positively for the rest of your life?

The psychologists have a law called the law of the group. That is, we associate with the people we see ourselves like. In other words, if you see yourself as weak, defeated, no future, then you are going to associate with people like that. But on the other hand, if you see yourself successful, reaching your goals, accomplishing dreams, going places in life, then you're going to associate yourself with successful, victorious, and achievers. Happy people hang around happy people; successful people hang around successful people.

If you want to know who you will be like in the future, take a good look at your friends. If your friends are all negative, always down, talking about their problems, that is not a good sign. Some people have friends who always dump their problem on them, which is going to poison you and affect your thinking. Your friend will be telling you how her husband ill treats her, and before long, you'll also say, "Is that how your husband treats you, then wait 'til you hear how mine treats me." If you have friends like this, then am afraid am going to advise you to evaluate your relationship and get new friends.

Who you associate with is whom you are going to be like. I want to encourage you to find somebody with the qualities you desire. Somebody that is doing what you want to do. Someone who has a bigger vision than you do and then stick with that person. Let their good qualities rub off on you. Watch their attitude, pay attention to how they treat other people, how they solve their problems, study their work habit and their determination. If you spend time with them, you are going to be like them.

I think about Elijah and Elisha in the Old Testament. Elijah was a great prophet of God. He was known for his mighty miracles. He was very powerful and a successful anointed man of God. Elisha was just an ordinary man. He saw the great works and miracles of Elijah. His attitude was "God you did it for him, and you can do it for me." He started hanging around him. He then said to himself, I want what he's got, and I will go everywhere he goes and find out what he is all about. He followed Elijah around and traveled with him wherever he went. When Elijah was leaving, he asked Elisha what he wanted, and Elisha said I want a double portion of your spirit. Elisha got twice the power and favor Elijah had. Moreover, today Elisha is known for twice the works Elijah did. That is what happens when you associate with the right people; you enlarge your portion.

Get some good Christian friends to hang around with. Find yourself an Elijah, somebody that has what you want, somebody you can look up to, people who will build you up and inspire you, not those who will tear you down. You can never soar with the eagle as long as you hang around the chicken.

Do associate yourself with the right people, who believe in bigger things, and your vision will be enlarged. If you associate yourself with people who have the favor of God, that favor is going to go all over you. You are going to get some of the qualities of the people around you.

Do not hang out with whoever comes your way; do not hang out with just anybody. You have to be selective in choosing who your friends should be. When you walk with wise people, you will be wise; when you walk with victorious people, you will be victorious yourself. Quit hanging around people who are lazy, not disciplined, and who are loose in morals. You are going to become like the people you constantly hang around. You hang around them, and you will be like them. Do not mingle with people who do not have anything you want. If they do not have peace, happiness, joy, victory, and are always depressed, then what is it that you want? Instead, encourage them to be the better person that they want to become.

What is around you is a portrait of what is inside you. What you respect, you will attract, not what you love. This is why people who work for worthy people could be broke. What you respect will come toward you. You cannot learn from someone you resent; you cannot learn from what you envy.

You can never outperform the portrait you have of yourself. Your conduct reveals how you feel of yourself. Your imagination plays a major role in your life. In your imagination, you are acting out an internal video of what you want to happen in reality.

We have to focus in life with what we want versus what we do not want. If you don't consciously decide what results you want to produce and represent things accordingly, then an external trigger, a conversation, a television show, a movie, whatever may create states that create behavior that do not support you.

It's important that we focus in life and act accordingly before it's late, for the great end of life is not knowledge but action;

and the ancestor of every action is a thought. The way we order the actions can make a huge difference in the kind of results we produce. "Let all things be done decently and in order" (1 Corinthians 14:40), which implies that if you have an agenda in life you must always fulfill it. We have to leave footprints here in this life, so that the generations that will follow will have easy access to information. We must pray to God to help us make a history and not to repeat a history in life.

We need to translate what we learn into reality. This is often not the case for the fear of making mistake. But then whatever humans have learned have to be learned as a consequence only of trial-and-error experience. Humans have learned only through mistakes.

Life is not perfect; not everything in life can be fixed. We as individuals have to be very conscious of ourselves, especially decisions that are taken by us. You cannot eat your cake and have it. The way you order the actions can make a huge difference in the kind of results we produce. We have to be productive in everything we do.

Life is not a problem to be solved, but a mystery to be lived. Just because things do not make sense to you does not mean that it does not make sense. Life is not ten miles good and twenty miles bad. Life has two roads, one good and the other bad. Nevertheless, both run parallel.

BELIEF, THE FOUNDATION OF EXCELLENCE

Faith takes strength, and it makes strength. Believe, and the burden will be lifted. Understanding and comfort will come. Begin to see the bigger picture, and the way is clear and bright again.

"Now faith is the substance of things hoped for, the evidence of things not seen. Through faith we understand that the worlds were framed by the word of God, so that things which are seen were not made of things which do appear. By faith Abel offered unto God a more excellent sacrifice than Cain, by which he obtained witness that he was righteous, God testifying of his gifts; and by it he being dead yet speaketh. By faith Enoch was translated that he should not see death; and was not found, because God had translated him; for before his translation he had this testimony, that he pleased God" (Hebrew 11).

These are written that ye might believe that Jesus is the Christ, the Son of God and that ye might have life through his name.—John 20:13

Christ lived the perfect life for us to be saved. He lived for nothing on his own; his was a life of love for other people. He gave himself a ransom for many. He came to do for us what we could not do for ourselves. He says in his word that if we are born twice, we die once; born once, die twice.

A belief is a strong emotional state of certainty that you hold about specific people, things, ideas, or experiences of life. You are what you think you are.

"Man is what he believes,"—*Anton Chekhov*

The word *Halloween* comes from All Hallows' Eve, which was the evening before a religious holiday in Medieval England that became known as All Saints' Day. It was a time set aside by the church to commemorate its saints.

Today's celebration of Halloween, however, is more closely related to pagan customs that originated in ancient Europe. The Druids believed that the spirits of the dead returned to their former haunts during the night of October 31, so they lit touches and set out food for these unwelcome visitors. They did this out of fear, thinking they would be harmed if they didn't.

The Bible warns against all dabbling in the occult and preoccupation with witches and ghosts. What then can Christians do? Yes, the example set by that great "cloud of witnesses" in Hebrews 12:1 encourages our faith. Remembering them on Halloween can remind us of the triumph of trusting the Lord.

Faith of our fathers, living still in spite of dungeon, fire, and sword, o how our hearts beat high with joy whenever we hear that glorious word!—*Faber*

Beliefs have a powerful effect on our lives. If you change the situation of how you represent something to yourself, you will change how you feel about it and thus change what is true in your experience of life.

Life is full of surprises. Though the doors to life open wide, and welcome whatever may come and look for the gift it brings and invite what is destructive to leave. Sometimes we lock the worst guest inside. Sometimes we get preoccupied with the hurt one may have caused us. And we are unable to get on with our life, and we nurse the pain so devoutly.

Anything in our world can change in an instant. And it's not just the boldface crises that defeat us. Any unwanted event we mentally replay will cost us our peace. Throughout our lifetime we will know anger, shame, fear, depression. Don't let them live with you. Open the door to faith. It's the guest you want to host forever. Let it fill your heart. Faith has always been sure shelter for mankind.

God never responds to our request; he responds to our faith. His only pleasure is to be believed; his only pain is to be doubted. What you make happen for others, God will make happen for you.

The world we live in is the world we choose to live in, whether consciously or unconsciously. If we choose bliss, that is what we get. If we choose misery, we get that too; therefore a belief in failure is a way of poisoning the mind. There is no such thing as failure. There are only results.

"There is nothing either good or bad, but thinking makes it so. Our doubts are traitors, and make us lose the good we oft might win, by fearing to attempt."—*William Shakespeare.*

Sometimes we learn from our mistakes, and the mistakes of others. Reflect on the "failures" in your life. What did you learn from those mistakes? I am sure they were some of the most valuable lessons you have learned in your life.

There is a time and a place for everything, and everyone and I truly believe that how you feel about yourself has a lot to do with your time and your peak. I am at a point in my life where I am feeling good about myself. I know there is always room for improvement, and quite honestly, I would never settle for "right now." To me, that would be stagnant, so I will always aim higher, try harder, and do better; and "hopefully," it will help me to become the better person I have always tried to be. I know my best days are just ahead because I know God is not through blessing me yet. I know today is the poorest I will ever be the rest of my life. The happiest days are just ahead.

THOUGHT

People are not enjoying life because their thought is a mess. Our life follow are thought. If you think negative, so will your life. You need to think about what you are thinking about; is it negative or positive?

To experience God's best, be careful of what your mind dwells on. You can choose your thought. The fact that something comes to mind does not mean you should dwell on it. You have a choice to think about it or not. It is important that you do not give negative thought the opportunity; get rid of it. The negative thoughts that feed on our mind could steal our destiny. Some negative thoughts such as "I will never make it," "I will never be wealthy." Do not dwell on it day after day; get rid of it immediately. You dwell on it and it gives you trouble. As it is written in Proverbs, as a person thinketh in his heart, so will he become.

What are you thinking? If you want to change your life, first change your thought. You could be your worst enemy, thinking negative stuff about yourself. Your own thinking could create a barrier. Get rid of these thoughts of insecurity. Keep your mind full of peace, harmony, joy, and happiness. Replace all the negative thoughts with positive thoughts. Replace it with the Word of God. Be bold and aggressive and replace it with God's Word. Our Lord and Father said in His Word that his blessings will chase us and fulfill us and nothing will be withheld.

The enemy cannot tell the truth; when he brings negative word to you, just turn it around and say the opposite of what he is telling you. When the devil says no, God says yes.

Think positive thoughts about your life. Set your mind on positive things. If you have a positive mind, you will have a positive life. When you are negative, you are in agreement with the enemy; and when you are positive, you are in agreement with God. Keep your mind on the higher things; keep your mind on victory. You need to quit thinking about how big your problem is. Keep your mind on the higher things. Your life will always follow your thoughts. Our emotions let us feel what we are thinking. Let go of the past. God will restore what the enemy has stolen. Check out on what you are thinking about. Get rid of the negative, discouraging thoughts. The mind is like a computer; what you store in it is what you get from it. If you think negative, you will never reach your potential. Your life is going to follow your thought. Keep God first place in your life.

SECTION II

The Gift Within

IDEAS

Do not underrate little things for great things come in small packages. God has put big in little, but people do not believe in little things. They always want to start big right from the beginning.

Ideas are internal. Many of the things we can see in substance are all by ideas, the computer, buildings, clothes, machines, etc. Ideas are free but very high to bring into being. Do not give up your dream; do not let go of the vision that you know. I know what men have taken away, God will restore. You should have all the energy you need to accomplish whatever is on your mind. Others may notice your enthusiasm.

When you have an idea about something, it could be music, or designing an invention, do not act immediately; instead keep the idea inside for a time. Saving yourself time and energy can help you feel better about all of your ideas. It's like cooking; you put the spices in; then you put the lid on for a while. Do not talk about your ideas; let them build up; it could be music, writing, painting, starting a new business, or designing an invention. Resist the temptation to talk to people about the idea or even to think about the result. You may be feeling quite energized, and if so, will want to tackle a variety of personal activities. Certain goals will require more than effort. Do not be over ambitious now. Pace yourself so that you do not try to do too much. In addition, be careful that you do not spread yourself too thin by trying to communicate your ideas with everyone around you.

Ideas are something nobody can steal from you, but then you have to put your ideas into being before you let it out, before you make it known to others, so they do not take it from you. When you have an idea about something, do not even think about the money you will make; just let it grow. Stay in the center of the high self, where the creative impulses arise if people around easily distract you; isolate yourself when the creative process is ongoing.

What is common to one is a mystery to the other. There are thousands of things in the Bible, but unless someone shows you, you will live a lifetime without knowing.

THE ANATOMY OF THE EARTH AND IDEAS

Genesis 3:19 tells us about the fall of man. The earth is pregnant with a lot of great things that can bring us ideas. Long ago, all around us was dust, but today what do we see? There are ideas that we cannot see. Everything we see around us use not to exist a one hundred years ago. Everything around us comes from the earth.

The earth is pregnant with resources that can take care of the future. We must desire not to let our backs to be covered. Our works must follow us, and we must look far into the future. We must create an enabling environment for prosperity, peace, joy, and happiness. Our ideas must fall into the soil and grow so that generations will continue with what we started with.

Ideas grow. When they are new, they are fragile. Certain things can destroy ideas. Ideas feed on words; they can grow as they find themselves at an atmosphere with the temperature that can make them grow. Words that are comforting, kind, encouragement, agreement. No idea comes out of you without the influence of your environment. When you nurse it well, it grows and gets wings and flies like an eagle. Education helps us to acquire the skills and information we need to make our ideas grow. Translate what you have learnt into reality.

Ideas come to us as individuals; if we don't take care of it, it will die before the release of a support. What ruin companies are ideas.

THEORY OF PATTERNS AND SCIENCE

God made us in his own image, so it means we look like him like in intelligence, ideas, and knowledge.

The inventor looks at the dynamics of a bird to make an airplane. The bird flies and moves around, moving from one country to the other, and so the scientist who happens to be a human being also thought of it to create a mechanism for one to move and travel as far as possible. So I guess the airplane was invented for us to travel to other countries like the bird does.

Bird

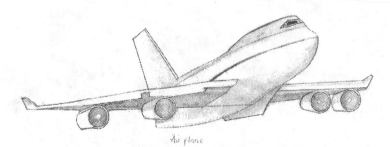

Air plane

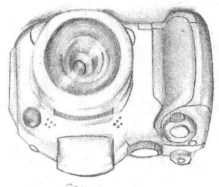

Camera

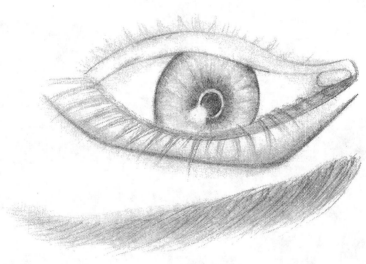

eye

Another example is the eye and the camera. God created the eye, and man invented the camera. The best way to understand how the eye works is to compare it to a camera. Both need light to see anything at all. Light surrounds us, usually traveling in straight lines. What the eye does, in the same way as the lens of a camera, is to bend the light in such a way that a perfect image is formed for us to see.

Parachute and umbrella can also be compared. To slow down a person or object falling from a great height, such as from an airplane. It increases the air drag around the falling body and stops it from being forced down too quickly by the force of gravity. The list can go on and on. In the early days, man was using his hands to eat before cutlery was invented. Charcoal was being used to clean the teeth before the toothbrush was invented; leaves and dry grass were being used to wash dishes before the dishwasher was invented.

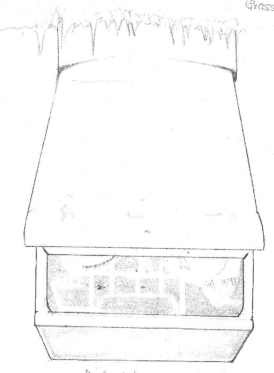

Grass

Dishwasher

In Africa, Water and Sewage Company can contact scientists to study how the heart functions, in supplying blood to the various parts of the body, so that it can be applied on how Africans are given or supplied water in their various homes.

Uninformed interference hinders our development. You have to know what you want in life before the opportunity comes. We have to have a purpose and know the path toward our destination. I look into nature, and I see a lot of life. God has given everyone the opportunity to make patterns. We must be able to hold it. Do not envy someone who has found his or her pattern. Dig deep in yourself and find yours. The laws, which can make life better for us, are always there. Look more in what is in existence.

SECTION III

The Ultimate Success

TRUE MEASURE OF SUCCESS IN LIFE

You're a success because of your choices on how to pursue your life's work.—*Beryl Hammond*

Many people living in their twilight years suddenly realize how empty and pointless their lives have been. They've made some successful business deals and had some fun, but in terms of satisfying friendships or lasting accomplishments, their lives have been zero. They have climbed the ladder of success, only to discover that all the while it had been leaning against the wrong wall.

As the apostle Paul looked back on his ministry, he saw that it had been rewarding but not easy. Measured by the world's yardstick of success, his life seems almost insignificant.

Paul wrote his second letter to Timothy while languishing in a cold, damp dungeon awaiting execution. In a matter of weeks, the apostle would stand before Nero, the half-insane emperor of Rome, and his life would end. But he knew that after his death he would receive the crown of life from the Kings of Kings. And we now know that the influence of his life changed the course of history itself.

An ancient historian would have written volumes about the splendor of Nero and probably never even mentioned Paul. Yet today we name our dogs Nero and our sons Paul. I guess what we live for is pretty important after all.

Jesus was born in a manger, a place so undignified for the Son of God, yet this did not change who he was or what he came to the world to do.

Joseph came from slavery, through the prison, to the palace, and yet he did not let his attainment in life cloud his judgment for him to forget his God who had delivered him and set him where he was.

David rose from being a shepherd boy in the bush tendering his father's sheep to become the king of Israel.

You can think your way to success with positive self-talk. Stop negative talk in its tracks and change it to positive talk. Replace negative talk (can't make it, am not good enough) with positive one (I can do it, I am smart), even if you don't think you are at your best; don't let that diminish your victories. If you work to maintain a bright vision of yourself, it will take you far along the road toward achieving your goals.

We need to apply whatever we learn, of the great branches of knowledge—the sciences, the social sciences, and the humanities. The sciences are applied, sometimes almost as soon as they are learned. Strenuous and occasionally successful efforts are made to apply the social sciences, but almost never are the humanities well applied. We do not use philosophy in defining our conduct. We do not use literature as a source of real and vicarious experience to save us the trouble of living every life again on our own.

"To laugh often and much; to win the respect of intelligent people and the affection of children, to earn the appreciation of honest critics and endure the betrayal of false friends; to appreciate beauty, to find best in others, to leave the world a bit better, whether by a healthy child, a garden path or a redeemed social condition, to know even one life has breathed easier because you have lived. This is to have succeeded."—*Ralph Waldo Emerson*

People who are able to produce outstanding results consistently produce a set of specific actions both mentally and physically. When I was in college, a very good friend of mine, Ayisha, approached me once after a lecture and said, "Beryl, how come you are able to score an A in even the very difficult subjects?" She then decided to join me whenever I am studying. She realized that I stayed up all night studying; she was like "Oh my god."

Another example is that of knowing someone who makes the greatest cookies in the world; can you produce the same quality results? Of course, you can, if you have the person's recipe. A recipe is nothing but a strategy, a specific plan of what resources to use and how to use them to produce a specific result. So what do you need to produce the same quality cookies as the expert baker? You need the recipe, and you need to follow it explicitly. If you follow the recipe to the letter, you will produce the same result or similar results. The baker might have worked through years of trial and error before finally developing the ultimate recipe. You can save years by following her recipe.

If you know what the ingredients are and how much to use, can you produce the same quality of cookies? No, not unless you know when to do what, and in what order. What if you put in first what the original baker put in last? You will not produce cookies of the same quality. If you use the same ingredients, in the same amounts, in the same sequence, then you will produce similar results if not the same results.

We all have the same potential resources available to us. It is our strategy that is how we use those resources that determines the results we produce.

Success is the ongoing process of striving to become more. It's the opportunity to continually grow emotionally, socially, spiritually, physiologically, intellectually, and financially while contributing in some positive ways to others.

The road to success is always under construction. It is a progressive course, not an end to be reached.

In life, there are strategies for everything—for motivation, for buying, for love, for being attracted to someone, seduction, learning, athletics, selling, efficient management, creativity; there are strategies for financial success, for maintaining good health, for staying slim, for looking beautiful, for feeling happy and loved throughout your life. Find people who are already successful or already have fulfilling relationships, just discover their strategy and apply it to produce similar results and save tremendous amounts of time and effort.

When Jesus came into the world, he identified himself with losers and those who had failed in life. He knew the great ones were losers before they were great. Jesus came to earth, so we could go to heaven; he became son of man, so we could become sons and daughters of God. He was born of the Virgin Mary, so we could be born again. God said that if you want to move forward in life, move backward; if you want to be great, be a servant; if you want to be first, be last; if you want to be wise, be a fool. (1 Corinthians 3:18) "If you want to be strong, be weak, if you want to be honorable, be despised."

Most people are unsuccessful in life not because they lack money, skill, or opportunity but because they are caught in a state of low being. Low being is a state of low energy, negative thinking, low self-esteem, blaming, and feeling sorry for oneself.

There are some things we all want in life, but sometimes we are not ready. The devil wants us to get it early. If you gain things quickly, you lose things quickly.

When you have a need for something, and you pray to God about it, there are two ways God can answer the prayer, either satisfying the need by providing you what you want or simply taking that need away. Example, you need a means of transportation to work every working day. God can either make it possible for you to buy a car, which will also boost your ego, or a friend can decide to offer you a ride to work every day; or better still, you can find yourself a job that is close to home. In either way, the need of transport is taken care of. There are no short cuts to our destiny. Do not be in a hurry to settle at your second best. Don't settle for silver, if you can have gold. Take one step at a time; stay open and be sensitive. Do things as soon as practicable rather than putting them off 'til later.

If you want to be successful and financially independent, you must commit yourself right now to ending your addiction to defeatist thinking and actions. Resolve right now to give up all blame and negative thinking. Think positive because your imagination plays a major role in your life.

"Begin at the beginning," the king said bravely, "then go till you come to the end; then stop."—Lewis Carol, in *Alice's Adventures in Wonderland*

Who you know, where you go, and what you own is not the true measure of personal success. Persistence is the difference between success and failure. In order to maintain a balanced self-image, you need to know how to cope with success and failure along the way.

It is not what happens to us that separates failures from success; it is how we perceive it and what we do about what happens that make the difference.

"The secret of success is making your vocation your vacation,"—Mark Twain.

There is no abiding success without commitment; it is the quality of commitment that separates good from great.

"To follow without halt, one aim; there is the secret of success,"—the great Russian ballerina, Anna Pavlova

Whatever it takes, it goes without saying you do whatever it takes to succeed without harming another person.

To succeed in life, sometimes you need to have enemies. This is so true. Enemies challenge us and hone our survival skills. They provoke our creativity and resourcefulness. Announce your goals, and enemies will show up. There are people in your life who are under satanic control. It could be your mother, father, siblings, friends, or enemy. We are born in a hostile environment. We must be conscious of the enemy. The size of your enemy determines the size of your reward. Do not enter a battle that does not offer a benefit. Sometimes when you delay a battle, you delay a reward. The devil uses those close to us to tempt us. Sometimes we are tempted to give up and stay the same. The prize is greater than the price. Yielding to temptation will not make you happy. It feeds you so that it makes you think that it will make you happy. It will only make you feel like you are a loser.

To be successful, we have to be obedient to God. When you ask God for a miracle, he will give you an instruction.

There is a question. Is success all about wealth, and is prosperity a material thing?

Prosperity is not only money, but peace, happiness, joy, knowledge, development, fairness, honesty, etc. Sin blocks prosperity; the scar it leaves is guilt. It can be forgiven, but it will pursue you. Check your concept of prosperity, since our concepts of prosperity influence us.

IS PROSPERITY ALL ABOUT WEALTH AND SUCCESS?

Biblical Concept of Prosperity

Old Testament Hebrew word for prosperity

Tsalach—To prosper, succeed, to be profitable, to advance, flourish, to be promoted. Literally means to pass over from failure to success. To satisfy satisfactorily what is intended. God is the source of *tsalach*. English meaning for tsalach is victory, triumph.

Sakal—To understand, to deal wisely, to be intelligent, prudent, knowledgeable, policy, intellectual abilities and skills, to deplore all the knowledge. What makes you prosperous and succeed, using all ideas and intelligence, Godliness, being wise, have insight, wisdom.

To whom who has *sakal* knows that to one problem there are many answers.

Halak—To travel, walk to and fro, go forward, proceed, run, journey, to spread, to advance, develop.

Tsedeq—Righteousness, justice and fairness, honesty, giving freely, benevolence without reward for gain.

Shamen—To be rich, fat, oiled, a word for prosperity conveys an idea of well-being, fertility land, nourishing (food).

Tov—Good, fineness, beauty, prosperity.

Shalom—Peace, ability to start a business and finish it, fulfillment of one's aspirations and ambitions in life, having a hygienic environment, wholeness, to be perfect, tranquility of mind and heart.

Barak—To bless, to knell.

CREATION AS AN ASPECT OF PROSPERITY

Things that God created are now producing their own kind. Everything he has produced is prosperous because it can reproduce. Prosperity is abundance. Man is body, soul, and spirit. When we want to prosper, every aspect must prosper. Physically and spiritually example, good health, energy, holiness. Man must be satisfied physically and spiritually, emotionally and mentally. We must progress and advance in our spirituality. In the beginning, God had a good relationship with man. Eternity has no beginning and end. Man's productivity and prosperity depends on the earth. Man has a very close relationship with the earth. God cursed the land after Adam and Eve sinned against God.

God has so many attributes and virtues. We must sit down and think about problems and find solutions to them, for we were created to succeed in whatever we lay our hands on. You must be number 1 in your own right. We need stability in our emotion. There should be emotional equilibrium, emotional balance.

There is enmity between nature and nature, nature and man, God and man, ever since man sinned. Nobody can make you happy, sad, or laugh until you want to be happy, sad, or laugh even though there are situations that could call for sadness, etc. Opportunity must come to understand the goodness of God.

Prosperity defines poverty, and poverty defines prosperity. We must be tactical and strategic in every step that we take. We must try to avoid certain people in life, example people who like undermining and criticizing all the time.